Handbook of

GEMSTONE CARVING

A COMPLETE GUIDE
TO THE
MATERIALS,
EQUIPMENT and
TECHNIQUES
FOR CARVING GEMSTONES

by

ED and LEOLA WERTZ

Copyright © 1968 by Gembooks
Latest printing with revisions 1994

ISBN 0-910652-06-6

Published by

GEM GUIDES BOOK COMPANY
315 Cloverleaf Dr., Suite F
Baldwin Park, CA 91706

Table of Contents

INTRODUCTION 4

CHAPTER 1
A REVIEW OF GEMSTONE CARVING 5

CHAPTER 2
GEMSTONES USED FOR CARVING 7
Test for Quality 7
Importance of Color 7
Hard and Soft Stones 8
Sources of Material 8

CHAPTER 3
IDEAS FOR SUBJECTS TO CARVE 9
Determining Size 9
Choosing a Subject 9
Sources of Ideas 9
Study and Observe 9
Recording Ideas 10
Interesting Stones 10
Templates and Models 10
Ceramics as Models 10
Modeling Clay 10
Knowing Your Subject 11
Challenging Subjects 11

CHAPTER 4
EQUIPMENT AND ITS USE 12
Function of Machines 12
Equipment Needed 12
Slabbing Saws 12
Coolants 13
Using Trim Saws 14
The Grinding Arbor 14
The Grinding Wheel 15
Equipment for Sanding . . . . 16.
Equipment for Polishing 16
The Carving Arbor 16
Custom Made Arbors 16
Commercial Arbors 18
The Drill Press 18
Electric Motors 20
Sources of Supply 20
Carving Costs 21
Workshop Space 21

CHAPTER 5
TOOLS AND HOW TO USE THEM 22
Mandrels 22
Small Grinding Wheels 22
Abrasive Points 23
Using Separating Discs 24
Diamond Tools 25
Sanding with Small Tools 25
Making Small Sanders 26
Rubber Bonded Wheels 27

Polishing 27
Small Hand Tools 27
Dust Control 28
Dop Sticks 28

CHAPTER 6
CARVING FORMS AND FINISHES 29
Carving Forms 29
Round or Flat? 30
Show Action 30
Blockiness 30
Features Without Color 30
The Appropriate Finish 31

CHAPTER 7
HOW TO CARVE A LEAF 32
The Drawing 32
Preforming 32
Grinding the Outline 33
Grinding the Features 33
Sanding 34
Finishing and Polishing 34

CHAPTER 8
CARVING IN THE ROUND 35
MOTHER AND BABE 35
Using a Model 35
Drawing the Image 35
Preforming With a Saw 35
Shaping With a Saw 36
Shaping With a Grinder 37
Redrawing the Image 37
Shaping With Small Tools 38
Sanding 39
Polishing 40
THE SPICE MERCHANT 40
A JADE VASE 41
Drilling a Carving 41

CHAPTER 9
PORTRAITS IN STONE 43
Choosing a Likeness 43
Studying the Subject 43
Laying Out the Work 43
Transfering the Image 43
Sawing 44
Grinding 44
Using Small Tools 44
Developing Details 45
Sanding and Polishing 45
Comments 45

CHAPTER 10
SOME NOTES ABOUT DISPLAY 46
Display Area 46
Crowding 46
Display Fixtures 46

APPENDIX 48

A bowl of grapes by Dr. Charles Irvin, DVM, Yucaipa California. The compote is howlite, the grapes are amethyst and the leaf is pale lavender jadeite.

The purpose of this book is threefold:

1. To create more interest in and understanding of gemstone carving and to promote the active participation of those who desire to start carving as a hobby.

2. To assist in the selection of suitable equipment, tools and material.

3. To present a workable plan with which to start and to acquaint you with carving procedures to a point where you can design and execute work in your own way.

Study and research has, no doubt, influenced the pattern of experiences in our own shop. Yet, as in any endeavor, the work pattern and products are also altered and shaped by the individuals directly involved. Through this combination of continued study and work experiences, various methods and procedures have been established. It is primarily on these that this book is based.

Many requests have been made that we share our accumulation of carving experiences. This indicates a need for such a work, particularly in the realm of how to start. We started as you may start — with no lapidary experience, no artistic ability, or training in this field. At that time there was meager information on equipment and procedure. Yet, it has been a most rewarding adventure.

An attempt has been made to provide information that will be u s e f u l. Throughout these pages we have tried to anticipate and answer the unasked questions that are sure to arise.

We believe, also, that it may benefit the reader who never plans to carve a stone. As more and more people become interested in working at this craft, you will see an increase in the number and quality of carvings. To know something of the way that a rock is transformed into a beautiful carving greatly increases your understanding and interest in what you see. This knowledge can aid in the evaluation of gem carvings as well.

With this in mind, please share with us the time required to read this small book. It may lead to an activity of lasting interest and pleasure for you.

Chapter 1

A Review of Gemstone Carving

A gemstone carving is time preserved: many efforts requiring time leave no evidence.

In substance, a gemstone carving already exists in a suitable piece of material. Its form, first a mental image, is released by the controlled removal of excess material.

In application and procedure we are concerned mainly with three phases in carving. First, we decide on a suitable subject; a form which we want to carve. Next, we select suitable material for the proposed subject. The carving is then fashioned by reducing the material to the desired form.

Our aim is to break down these steps to an understandable, workable plan. Only in a completed carving do the different steps of development come into focus and become one.

Qualifications

First of all, let's banish the common notion that only the very talented or those with artistic training can qualify to start carving. Without doubt, these attainments would be a big help and make parts of the procedure more simple and easy. And, very likely, they would produce a better finished product.

The one requirement necessary to this craft is *desire. The desire to carve.* Without it, talent or artistic ability won't dent a stone. Without a desire to carve, it would be impossible to have the patience required to execute an intricate carving, for many hours of work are involved. But for one with the desire and determination for self-expression through the medium of gemstone carving, the lack of patience ceases to be a factor. You'll likely regret that even more time can't be devoted to it.

Use of Time

By its very nature, carving is time consuming. The necessity of using small tools on hard stone creates this factor. But each of us have at least some leisure time beyond that required for work, rest and worship. Free time plus effort

can equal a beautiful carving for lasting enjoyment. Carving is also a fine stepping stone to bridge the gap from our productive years into the abundance of time available in retirement.

Lapidary Experience

It's not essential that you have a background of lapidary experience, though this training is helpful in several ways. For one, you will be familiar with the tools and equipment. Perhaps it should be explained that all of the needed equipment, except the carving arbor and possibly a drill press, is used in routine lapidary work. The majority of people who have contacted us with a desire to carve have at least some lapidry experience. So we'll not give detailed information on the use and care of conventional equipment, but rather as it pertains to carving. A number of excellent books are available on general lapidary techniques. These may be bought at most rock shops or through the gem and lapidary magazines.

Although step by step information may become dull reading for those who are advanced, we supply it here for the beginner to whom any part of gemstone carving is complicated.

It isn't important what subject you choose for your first carving. Nor is the choice of material too important. But getting started is important. With some people there seems to be a barrier at this point. They have arranged for material and equipment and have enough know-how to start. Yet they wait. Here are a few suggestions if this tends to be a problem for you.

Don't start with the idea that your first attempt must turn out perfectly. Accept the fact that it is a craft that takes time and determination to learn. Use good material but not a stone that you especially prize. Follow the instructions in Chapter 7 as a starter. But, thereafter carve what interests you and offers a challenge in the making. The result will be more rewarding.

5

Carving Examples

In Chapter 7 we've outlined initial steps in making a leaf and various helps in other carvings. You may not like a leaf, yet the mechanics of the procedure remain essentially the same if you choose another subject. The objective is to acquaint you with the use of the equipment. If you learn its use with the simple cuts, its operation later becomes automatic. Then full attention can be devoted to shaping more advanced carvings.

A Comparison

In comparison to other classes of the lapidary work, carving has advantages as well as disadvantages. No other phase of the hobby allows more freedom of design and use of the imagination in carrying out the plan. There is greater opportunity for self-expression in the finished work.

Yet, because of this freedom, there is no precise guide to follow, so it offers a real challenge. When you plan to do a carving, you start with one of two things: a stone to which you must fit an idea (Fig. 1) or an idea for which you must find a stone (Fig. 2). You have no prepared templates, no set of angles to follow, no directions for execution. You don't follow a plan, you build a plan.

To the veteran carver this never ceases to offer a challenge. Nor does a completed carving completely satisfy the desire to create. More nearly, it is a stepping stone to a more challenging subject and a more fulfilling experience.

Fig. 2. A long search was made before rhyolite with a suitable combination of colors was found for this subject. It is one piece, the hands about 4 ½ inches long.

Chapter 2

Gemstones Used for Carving

Good quality material is of prime importance in carving. Select a stone free of fractures or pits. A tough stone, as opposed to a brittle one, is very desirable. For this reason jade has been a leading material with carvers for many years. But many other stones have been used and are also suitable. Among them are jasper, agate, howlite, travertine, serpentine, rhodonite, chert, quartz crystal, rhyolite, obsidian, and opal.

Selecting Material

Although these and many more can be carved with success, the design of the proposed carvings should help you determine the nature of the material to be used. If there are to be fragile areas that project from the main body of the carving, you should use a tough material such as jade. If the finished work can be supported as in Fig. 3, a delicate carving in obsidian can be done.

As you continue carving, likely you will use many different materials. Each has a place in regard to color, texture, and suitability to the subject.

Test for Quality

It's time well spent to try a stone with which you are not familiar before proceeding with a major project. Here is a good way to determine its usefulness: cut a cabochon or a simple leaf, paying close attention to brittleness while using the trim saw and grinding. Is the stone even in hardness or does it have soft spots? Does it undercut when being polished or have an orange-peel appearance when it is finished? Does it fracture easily from heat while being worked? Is the general appearance of the finished stone suitable for the carving you have planned?

Observing material in this way will help you select the proper one and will avoid disappointment in the finished work.

Importance of Color

As mentioned, jade has been extensively used for carving. One principal reason is its resistance to breaking. In this respect it is probably unsurpassed.

Many times, however, the desired color can't be obtained in jade and another material must be used. It is well to give serious thought to the color of the stone selected for a proposed subject. If we strive to duplicate the characteristics of shape and design, should we also not try to achieve the same in color and texture of finish? Of course, to match the color of the original subject is not always possible. Avoid a clash of color or multiple colors that you would not expect to see in the subject.

We very seldom, if ever see a black flower in nature, so carving one would look unnatural. Yet, a black leaf may be substituted for green and if the texture of the finished material is suitable, it will attract little notice.

A stone with straight parallel bands or layers can often be used to good advantage. It is sawed parallel to the bands when used for cameo or portrait work. One or more layers can be used to show contrast of color and thus separate the figure from the background. If the layers are thin and the colors are distinct,

Fig. 3. This garland of leaves is carved from one piece of obsidian, about 4 1/2 inches high. The first cut from a rock produced this slice with a hole in otherwise solid material. The carving was designed to fit the stone. A mounting of gold plated metal supports the carving.

they also may be used to show the color of hair or clothing, with another layer used for the face.

Brightly patterned or multicolored stone can be used for some carvings such as bowls or vases. More often, however, material of one or two colors or with a gradual gradation of color can be used to better advantage.

Light colored, translucent stone also may fail to show fine lines or other detail necessary to clearly portray the subject. A simple experiment with a small piece of the proposed stone should be made. This can be examined under different lighting conditions before proceeding with a major project.

Hard and Soft Stones

There is a wide range in hardness in the stones that can be used for carving. They vary from very soft to extremely hard. The principal advantage of working with softer stones is that excess material can be more quickly and easily removed. The comparable value of a carving in soft stone or hard stone may be a matter of personal opinion. The material used may be of small concern if it is viewed solely from an artistic standpoint. Yet, to an experienced carver the object cut from a hard or difficult stone would find favor.

If the finished carving is to have fine detail, it can be accomplished much better with a hard, tough stone. For the beginner or inexperienced cutter, a stone that is not too soft is advised. It is less likely to be overground and progress of the work can be observed better.

Source of Material

Gemstone of adequate size, quality, and desired color is not always readily available. Plain colors are often needed and may be difficult to find. Material of this kind is often considered unsatisfactory for most rock work and, therefore, not stocked by supply houses.

You are fortunate if you live in an area where you can hunt for rocks. The one your partner passes up as too plain may be just what you need for your next project.

It is advisable to keep future needs in mind when looking over a stock of material. Many rock shops and lapidary supply houses have good material for sale. Dealers at most of the rock shows have a variety of good material from which to choose. The leading magazines also have many advertisements of gemstones for sale.

Fig. 4. This quartzite leaf is one of the author's first carvings.

Fig. 5. The beautiful rainbow colors in Brazilian agate prompted the design for this fish. The mounting is natural coral.

Chapter 3

Ideas for Subjects to Carve

The question most asked by people viewing your display of carvings is, "Where do you find the patience?" This was briefly discussed in Chapter 1. A close second to the first question is. "Where do you get all your ideas for subjects to carve," To the beginner this can be somewhat of a problem, so it will be discussed.

To Determine Size

Since there is no set pattern of instruction or plans to follow, the subject and execution of the plan for a subject must be yours. Where it is practical, a carving may duplicate the size of the subject after which it is patterned. A leaf is an example. But, more often, due to the size of a stone, free of fractures, and a lack of equipment to handle larger stone, carvings are in miniature compared to the dimensions of the original subject. So, there is no barrier as to the size of a subject to use as a model. The controlling factor is the size of the stone you can obtain and handle.

Choosing a Subject

We have all the world from which to select a subject. Pick an item you like and are interested in. If you like gardening, trees, and flowers; try making a leaf as shown in Fig. 4. Other hobbies or interests will suggest ideas which you may like to carve. See Fig. 5. But start on a subject you like, for you will be more willing to stay with it when you become discouraged (yes, you may at times) and enjoy more the completed work.

Source of Ideas

Ideas for carving projects may be obtained from pictures in magazines, nature books, calendars, or any similar source. As a rule no single picture will be a design you will use, but it will suggest an idea to you. You may incor-porate ideas from two or more pictures to complete a design. See Fig. 6.

It is advisable to collect and file any material you see. It may be of interest later on. These pictures may include animals, humans, hair styling, folds of robes or clothing, action pictures, and many, many more.

Reasonably priced paperback books are available covering many aspects of sketching and drawing. These can be obtained at most art and book stores and can be a big help to those with no training in this field. This probably includes most of us seeking to learn carving. But this does not imply that you must become expert at drawing. In the course of a year of carving, you may be required to design and draw only a few subjects. Find the help you need when you need it and don't let unforeseen problems bother you.

Study and Observe

Learn to observe what you see about you in your home, place of work, and in all natural things. It is amazing what we see repeatedly around us and yet know little about. As a subject is studied with the intention of reproducing it in stone, it takes on a different and magnifieid meaning. Here are a couple of examples:

We recently gave assistance in learn-

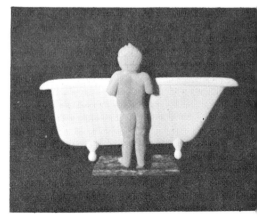

Fig. 6. Three individual carvings make up this picture: the child, the tub, and the rug, all done in flat work.

9

ing to carve to a man seventy years of age. After some instruction and some time had elapsed, we accepted an invitation to his home to see the progress of his work. As we approached the house, he and his wife were just returning from a walk around the block. The autumn leaves were falling in abundance and he had selected several with fine color and character. His first words were not the usual form of greeting. With almost a guilty look on his face, he remarked, "You know, Mrs. Wertz, I never really saw a leaf until I started to carve one from stone."

We, everyone, to some extent, has the same failing. We still have a letter on the desk from a lady in another state. She had written thanking us for a leaf carved from fossil ivory. To illustrate a point, she said, in part:

"The ivory leaf is simply beautiful. The flow of the curve really captures a rhythm. I looked out my living room window at the orange leaves and noted how curved and curled they were — not just flat with no movement . . ."

This observation is not confined to leaves; it pertains not only to carving. We can all broaden our horizons by simply observing.

You probably will become interested in researching some of the subjects you plan to do. This is a phase of the hobby that is also enjoyable. As this observation and study is followed for a while, it becomes natural to associate what you see around you with the possibility of fitting it to a plan for a carving.

Record Ideas

Many things will suggest ideas or arrangements during your regular routine. When this occurs, record it in some way, either by a sketch or written description of the idea. Or, if time permits, make a start on the project with the stone.

This is important for several reasons. As you work on a major carving which may require a long period of time, it is relaxing to change to another subject of less importance. In fact, several carvings of a different nature may be worked intermittently with good re-

sults. When working on one too long and too closely, the overall picture sometimes becomes obscure because of concentration on one part. Also, when all effort is centered on one carving at a time, when completed, it is usually difficult to quickly and easily select another subject unless it has already been recorded.

Interesting Stones

In a collection of stones several may suggest some special use by their shape or other characteristic. You may instantly think of an idea or form for a certain stone. Or, perhaps, you recognize a possibility but no definite plan presents itself. Then it is advisable to place a few of these stones where you can occasionally study them as you go about your work. The place isn't important as long as you have an opportunity to glance at them or perhaps study them for a few minutes from time to time. Ideas for a specific stone often come suddenly or when you are not concentrating on it at all.

Templates and Models

The selection or creation of patterns and models for this craft requires considerable planning and effort. It's much easier to work from a model in three dimensions than from a picture or drawing. Measurements can then be taken and transferred to the layout on the stone. Therefore, it is advisable to collect and save items which may be of use for this purpose.

Good replicas of leaves and flowers are available in plastic. If you wish to preserve a natural leaf or flower, dip it in melted paraffin wax. Don't have the paraffin hot; use only enough heat to melt it. This will preserve the natural contour and form of the leaf and offer a good working model.

Ceramics and Models

Ceramics can sometimes be used as models but avoid one that tends to be blocky. Where a ceramic is painted to project certain areas, the carving without the color may lack much of the character of the model.

Modeling Clay

Modeling clay is useful for preparing a subject to duplicate in stone. It has an advantage over nonplastic materials in that pieces can be put back if too much is removed. Making a model usually requires building up and removing before a suitable form is made. But the time isn't wasted; it acquaints you better with the subject you plan to work. Measurements, too, can then be transferred and drawn directly on the stone to be cut.

A carving in the round should be designed for strength and for character. A slender, fragile projection from the main body of a carving should be avoided. If it sticks out, design the carving so the projection can be anchored at the free end.

The simplest of designs for a carving in the round is fine for a starter. But thereafter, strive for a balance between one so complicated that the amateur's tools can't complete it and one so simple it has an assembly line appearance. Strive for individual character in each carving.

Know Your Subject

The experienced carver has found that the preliminary work involved in preparing a model or drawing is time well spent. First, it provides measurements to work from. But more than this, it acquaints you in detail with your subject.

Let's use, for example, a portrait. If a picture is used as the model, then several drawings are required before work can be started on the stone. It is first drawn by placing a thin transparent paper over the picture. This image is then transferred by carbon paper to the stone. So that the markings don't erase easily, it is retraced again with an aluminum pencil. With each drawing you become more familiar with the subject. It all helps when actual work is started on the stone.

Another incident comes to mind. Several of the portraits in our display were drawn directly on the stone. These were simply faces to portray a certain human character or race of people. On two or three of these, small errors were made in the drawing. They were not important enough to change, we thought, but important enough to notice and make a mental note to correct as the stone was being carved. But the amazing thing was that the completed carving still looked like the original drawing.

So it is a big help to study your subject. A bit of research in an encyclopedia or other reference often helps. Any correction or change should be made on the drawing or model before the carving is started. Then the cutting of the stone can be done more readily rather than by feeling your way as you work.

This is your homework. Study it well and your work will be easier and your carving better.

Challenging Subjects

To become skilled in gemstone carving one must observe, study, and practice. It requires a gradual advancement to more difficult and intricate subjects. Truly, as we grow in experience, the impractical project becomes difficult and the difficult becomes easy. A carving that seems entirely out of our range of ability may later be approached with full confidence. The skill required to fashion the carving has remained the same, we have grown to meet the challenge.

Recently, our small son made a statement parallel to this. Some time ago he had enjoyed watching the dishwasher being loaded from his vantage point on a chair. After ignoring the procedure for a few months, he walked by again. As he looked on he exclaimed, "Look, Mom, the dishwasher is down where I can see inside now!"

So it is with carving. Eventually the out-of-reach comes down to our size.

Chapter 4

Equipment and Its Use

Function of Machines

Generally speaking, the equipment and tools associated with gem carving are used for three purposes: to remove excess material, to develop detail, and to sand and polish. The machine accomplishes only what the operator asks of it, for the stone is applied freehand to the tool being used. The machine itself does not shape nor fashion a carving in any sense.

Many people, however, upon seeing our carving arbor, said they had a vague idea of carving being done by some expensive, fantastic machine. Some expressed the thought that the machine was "set" to perform the cutting of an individual carving. And, almost without exception, they show surprise at the simplicity of the equipment used to carry out this work.

This concept is easy to understand. Only a very small percentage of lapidaries do extensive carving in stone. So there is little publicity and not many carvings to see, other than imports, and little else to direct thought or study to this field.

Equipment Needed

Conventional lapidary equipment is used for much of the work. This includes a slabbing saw, trim saw, grinding arbor, belt or drum sander, and a polishing arbor. One additional piece of equipment is necessary — a carving arbor or a motor tool with which small points and discs can be used for detail work. A drill press is needed for carving vases, dishes, or similar items which require drilling or internal shaping.

In describing all of the machines that are useful in the carving process, we do not want to create the impression that you must have all of them. For instance, whether or not you have a large slab saw is only a matter of convenience. Many carvers have worked only with a small trim saw. A drill press is handy if you must drill a vase but completely unnecessary for most carving projects. Actually, it is possible to carve with

only a simple carving arbor and its accessories. What you add to this basic tool is a matter of your own desire, convenience, and pocketbook.

Sawing slices, of course, is the basic use of the slabbing saw. While 3/16 inch is the standard thickness for cabochon work, the sculptor will discover there is no standard of thickness. Each project may require a special cut, shape or thickness.

The slabbing saw can be used for much of the preliminary work of a carving in the round. A rough rock can be cut to the desired shape, such as a square or rectangle. Sawing is often necessary as a test to determine the consistency of pattern or color and to check the quality of a stone. A new cut may sometimes expose a fracture otherwise obscured and prevent disappointment later.

A series of closely spaced parallel cuts is often used to eliminate excess material. The thin portions left between the cuts can be easily broken out with a screwdriver or similar tool. We have used this method in the slabbing saw and controlled the depth of the cut by accurately timing the starting and stopping of the saw. A trial run must be made on another rock to determine the time needed for a certain depth of cut. This method, of course, requires strict supervision to prevent sawing too deeply.

Figures 7, 8, and 9 show how waste material may be removed with the slabbing saw for a carving in the round. This temporary, vertical, extension of the vise allows the stone to pass over the top of the blade, thus making a cut of uniform depth from one side of the stone to the other. This, in effect, works the same as an ordinary table saw used for cutting lumber. The vise, rather than a table, holds the material to be cut but it travels over the blade for a uniform depth of cut. The depth and the angle of the cut are determined by the position of the rock in the vise.

Fig. 7 A temporary, vertical vise extension can be made from pieces of 3/4-inch plywood with a spacer at the bottom of the vise. The thickness of the rock controls the size of the spacer.

Fig. 8. Move the stone and vise to the side of the blade to determine the depth of the cut.

Fig. 9. The cross feed is used to position the stone horizontally. Angles may be cut by properly positioning the stone. Be sure the stone is secure in the vise.

Fig. 9A. Attachments such as this allow controlled depth cutting by passing the work over the blade. It can also position the stone in an almost limitless variety of other positions. It can be used with either slab or trim saws.

The cross feed is used to set the horizontal position. Also, see Fig. 9A.

This arrangement may present the problem of not allowing the lid to close on your saw. If so, fasten a strip of canvas or plastic on the outside of the lid and drape it inside the saw chamber to prevent oil splash.

An alternate method for this type of sawing is to temporarily install a smaller diameter blade on the shaft and thereby eliminate the vise extension. Additional oil would be needed in the saw chamber with this arrangement.

Each carving is likely to present a slightly different problem when removing the unwanted stone. But the diamond saw is the answer for the removal of the mass of waste material.

Sawing can be obtained commercially. The cost is based on the square inches of surface to be cut.

Coolant

A coolant is always used with a diamond blade to lubricate and prevent overheating of the blade and the stone. A light oil such as Shell's Pella or Texaco's Almag Ethylene Glycol may be used for this purpose. The oil in the saw is maintained at a level that permits the blade to dip into and carry the coolant to the stone being cut.

Recommended speeds and other necessary instructions are furnished with new equipment. Follow them carefully to obtain the best service.

13

Using the Trim Saw

As the name implies, the trim saw is designed primarily for trimming away unwanted material. A common use is to saw out a marked pattern from a slice of stone. This is necessary in carving as well as other lapidary work.

Start by holding the slice of stone firmly on the trim saw table and, with a little pressure, let it feed evenly. Leave a narrow margin outside the marked line which is later removed with a grinding wheel. Continue sawing until the pattern is blocked out in straight cuts.

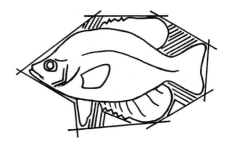

Fig. 10. Remove material from restricted areas by making short, parallel cuts with a trim saw. Break out thin sections between cuts.

When trimming to sharply curved lines on flat work, it is often necessary to saw straight parallel cuts into the restricted area as shown in Fig. 10. Remember that the blade will make a deeper cut on the underside of the slice. The amount depends on the diameter of the blade as well as the thickness of the slice. Allowance must be made for this difference if you are sawing toward, rather than parallel to, a marked outline or form.

This undercutting can be corrected by stopping the saw cut with allowance made for the additional travel on the underside of the slice. Then turn the slice over and cut slightly to compensate for the difference.

An alternate way to eliminate this sawing problem is to make a jig which, in effect, is an auxiliary table on the regular trim saw blade. The device consists of a wooden wedge with a slot in which the saw blade travels. It is designed with an angle that allows the slice of stone to feed toward the center of the blade to eliminate undercutting.

We find a husky .040 or .050 blade more durable and satisfactory for the tough jobs encountered in gem carving. It is a common practice in our shop to use the trim saw blade as a grinding wheel, i.e., to manipulate the stone in various positions against the blade. It is effective and fast. But the watchword here is caution and know-how. If possible, rest some portion of the stone on the saw table and hold it firmly with both hands. Use the blade to take off surface material, not to make a deep cut. Move it sideways as you grind or saw shallow criss-cross or parallel cuts close together. If a stone is not positioned solidly on the saw table, that is, if it is held free-hand or partially so, no single cut should be deeper than the thickness of the blade. If the cut is too deep, a slight movement of the stone can jam the saw blade, causing minor damage, hurt fingers or both.

Most trim saws are equipped with a vise designed to hold rocks as they are fed into the saw to be sliced. The larger trim saws can be used to some extent in this way if a slabbing saw is not available. Before you buy, however, check to see if the saw will cut stones as large as you want to work.

The trim saw is a versatile tool. Use it where possible in preforming a carving. The irregular, rough surface is then smoothed on a grinding wheel of suitable size.

The Grinding Arbor

One or more arbors are necessary for use in the grinding operation. The size of the grinding wheels determines the size of the arbor shaft needed. Arbors designed for grinding are equipped with a guard or shield over the wheel. This is a necessary safety device and also serves as a splash guard for the water coolant which is necessary at all times when grinding stone.

If a permanent setup is to be made, water can be supplied through a small copper tube and controlled to a drip or spray directly on the grinding wheel. Trays beneath the wheels then catch excess water which may be drained or emptied.

A method commonly used is simply a pan of water containing a sponge placed under the grinding wheel. When in use, the sponge is raised to touch the wheel with enough pressure to keep an even distribution of water on the cutting surface of the wheel. This arrangement is quite satisfactory and simple. Use a bit of caution here — always remove the sponge when not in use. Otherwise, the wheel will become out of balance due to absorbed water in only one area.

The number of arbors you employ is principally a matter of convenience. Grinding wheels should be mounted on one arbor and left undisturbed. This is advisable because of the danger involved if a wheel should be damaged or broken by constant handling or repeated installation.

The Grinding Wheel

A silicon carbide or diamond grinding wheel is used in shaping and carving and smoothing the cuts left by the diamond saw blade. If only one wheel is employed, a 100-grit, 8-inch diameter wheel is practical for ordinary work. Many cutters use a finer grit wheel, also, to remove coarse grinding marks left by the 100-grit wheel. A drum sander equipped with either 120- or 220-grit cloth has worked well in our shop for this purpose, however.

A grinding wheel one inch thick is

Fig. 11. This spinning wheel was made from slices of petrified wood with only a trim saw and an 8-inch grinder.

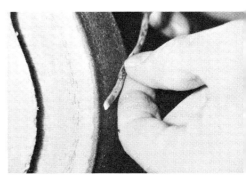

Fig. 12. The stem of a flower being ground. Use the thumb and the finger to support the stone where it contacts the wheel to prevent breakage.

satisfactory because the corners of the wheel get, by far, the hardest use. This makes it necessary to frequently dress the silicon carbide wheel to keep it true and the corners square. Grinding wheel speed is important. Follow the instructions furnished with each wheel.

If the work of carving was to be divided into three divisions — preforming with the diamond saw, grinding, and finishing — the grinding would be the longest job on most carvings. It is the time consuming grinding that leads to the final shape of the carving. The tools may range in size from an 8-inch grinding wheel to a mounted point no larger than the point of a lead pencil. The skill of the operator to visualize the image and to properly use the equipment to develop it determines the caliber of the carved form.

Perhaps the first thing to stress is to use the largest grinder possible on a given job. Use it as long as any material can be removed without endangering areas that must be left unground. Then change to a smaller tool, but, if conditions permit, return again to the larger grinder; it's faster and cheaper. The spinning wheel shown in Fig. 11 was made with only a trim saw and an 8-inch grinding wheel to fashion the various parts.

Small, fragile areas of a carving should be supported with a finger or thumb directly behind the fragile area being ground. In fashioning stems for a flower arrangement, as shown in Fig. 12, we ground, sanded, and polished obsidian to a 1/8-inch diameter, over three inches long with this method.

Equipment for Sanding

Conventional as well as diamond belt, drum, and disc sanders are employed when the design of the carving permits their use. Many carvings can be sanded in some areas, at least, with this equipment. The balance of the carving is then sanded with small tools which are discussed in Chapter 5.

Three grades of sanding cloth are needed for a complete sanding job. By mounting each size on a separate drum, they can be used on one arbor and then changed as the need arises. It is time consuming and the end of the cloth will sometimes break with repeated change. But more important is the tendency to slight the sanding job when convenient facilities are not available.

Sanding cloth is available to be used dry only or wet-or-dry. The latter is preferred in our shop even though it may be used dry at times. There may be special cases but for general use 220-, 440-, and 600-grit cloth meets most requirements. With diamond tools follow the manufacturer's recommendations for grit sizes.

In Fig. 13 a drum sander is being used to finish a carving of a bird. Note how the carving is being held to the edge of the sanding cloth. This is often necessary to prevent destroying the de-

tail of an adjacent part of the carving. Both edges of the sander can be used and the carving at times must be held to the sander in many different positions to get to all areas. Many items can be sanded on the regular equipment with some practice.

A word of caution. Drum sanders vary in their construction beneath the periphery of the wheel, i.e., the hub, spokes, or cloth-tightening apparatus may hit some portion of the carving as it is being maneuvered into different positions. Use care, especially with subjects that have projecting areas that may be easily broken.

Equipment for Polishing

Wheels for polishing can be mounted with an adapter directly to the motor shaft or on a lightweight arbor. Slower speeds are required than for grinding and sanding and the wheels are much lighter.

Most commonly used for polishing are leather, muslin, or hard felt wheels. We are speaking here of conventional equipment which is used anytime conditions permit. When the size and shape of the carving requires smaller tools, they are usually made of the same materials in sizes to fit the job. These small tools and their use are described in Chapter 5.

The Carving Arbor

When all excess stone has been removed that is possible by conventional sawing and grinding, it becomes necessary to use smaller tools to finish the shaping of many carvings. Commonly used for this purpose is a simple arbor with a chuck attached to the shaft which holds the required tools. These may vary in design as each machine has been developed individually to serve a need.

Custom Made Arbors

A custom made arbor may be built or assembled with standard available parts. To be successful it must provide a variation of speed, either by a variable speed motor or by multiple step pulleys. The latter works well if provision is made

Fig. 13. The edge of a drum sander being used to finish a carving. Smaller tools were used to work the neck, part of the head, and below the wings.

Fig. 14. This home built carving arbor has worked well in the authors' shop for many years. A separating disc is being used here to cut veins in a leaf. Photo by Marvin Monroe, Nampa, Idaho.

for easy changing from one pulley to another. The shaft must run smoothly without vibrating.

A collet chuck is advised. Because of its smaller diameter it offers less interference as a stone is being worked. The carving arbor shown in Fig. 14 has served well for many of the carvings shown in this book. It has required little attention. On this arbor provision is made for using medium-sized tools and buffs on the end of the shaft opposite the chuck. This provides a more versatile machine. A 1/2-inch by 4-inch grinding wheel, a 6-inch felt buff, and a 4-inch leather polishing wheel, alternately used at this position, eliminated the necessity of an additional arbor.

Another design eliminates this feature and uses only the chuck-end of the shaft. Although arbors of this type vary, a common feature enables the shaft to be tilted downward. In use the operator faces and looks down on the end of the shaft and tool. This arrangement is considered by some to offer a better view when working fine detail. However, if grinding wheels up to 1 inch in diameter are to be used, we find advantage with the arbor in a horizontal position. The stone is held to the wheel in the same manner as one being ground on a larger wheel.

An important feature of any carving arbor is to have sufficient clearance to freely move and turn the stone being worked. There should be a minimum of 3 inches of unobstructed area from the arbor bearing or mounting to the outer end of the chuck. With the mandrel or tool installed, ready for use, a distance of approximately 4 inches is obtained. If the arbor shaft is to remain in a horizontal position, it should be about 4 inches above the table top. This provides a comfortable rest for the arms and still allows clearance for handling the stone. See Fig. 15.

A shaft of 1/2-inch diameter is suitable for this arbor. Smooth running and longer life are obtained by using sealed ball bearings. These can be obtained in self-aligning, pillow blocks

Fig. 15. A comfortable arm rest and sufficient clearance to freely manipulate the stone contribute to both enjoyment and efficiency of the work. Extra large carvings may require more clearance. Note in this example that both horizontal and vertical clearance is at least 4 inches.

Fig. 16. Three-step pulleys make speed changes quick and easy. A quick change of arbor speed is possible with this pulley arrangement.

which are easily mounted. A three step pulley on both the motor and the arbor shaft will provide a suitable range of speed. This will range from 600 or 700 to 5,000 rpm. In assembly, place the step pulley on the arbor in the opposite direction to the motor pulley as shown in Fig. 16. Thus the belt length can remain constant at any speed setting without moving the motor.

The foregoing discussion on carving arbors has dealt entirely with do-it-yourself or custom made machines. This practice was established by those who pioneered in the field of amateur carving. There was a need for a machine and none were commercially available. Therefore, the need was individually met by experimenting and building a machine that best fit their need.

Commercial Arbors

Today, however, machines are available as combination units used for drilling, buffing, and small carvings. Some of these units, shown in Figs. 17, 18, 19, 20, and 21, feature a rheostat to control motor speed. These machines, of course, have the advantage of being already assembled and ready to operate. Prices and detailed information can be obtained from your lapidary dealer.

Another machine long used in the lapidary and jewelry field is the motor driven flexible shaft. See Fig. 20. This can be obtained as a complete unit or only the flexible shaft and hand piece can be bought to be used on your own motor or drill press. Equipment of this kind is used in a different manner than the arbor with a rigid shaft. In use, the stone is secured or held in a stationary position. The tool end of the flexible shaft is held in the hand to accomplish the desired results. With any type of rigid shaft machine, the working tool remains in a stationary position while the stone is held and moved by hand to the tool being used.

Some excellent carvings have been made with each type of equipment, and some craftsmen employ both types in order to better handle all phases of the work.

The Drill Press

A drill press can be used as a carving arbor by mounting it on 3/4-inch ply-

Fig. 17. The No. 605 Covington Diamond Drill motor can be swung to a horizontal position and both ends of the shaft used as a carving arbor. Courtesy Covington Lapidary Engineering Corp., Redlands, California.

Fig. 19. Tool rest from Contempo converts their machine to a specialized mini-lathe. Courtesy of Contempo Lapidary Equipment Co.

wood base, hinged so it can be lowered to a horizontal position as shown in Fig. 21. The usual speed range is from 500 to 5,000 rpm which is adequate. A piece of plywood (not shown) placed above the motor serves as an arm rest and also keeps grit from dropping into the motor. While this arrangement may have some disadvantages, one machine serves two purposes and thus offers a savings in initial cost. If work space is limited, this is also an advantage.

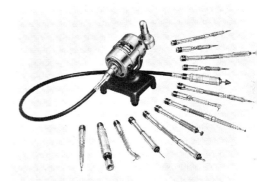

Fig. 20 The Foredom Miniature Power Tool with flexible shaft and a variety of interchangeable handpieces and chucks. Courtesy Foredom Electric Company, Inc., Bethel, Connecticut.

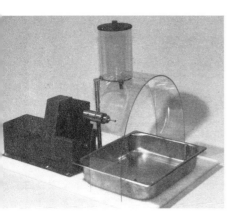

Fig. 18. This carving machine from Contempo uses water as a coolant and to help control dust. Courtesy Contempo Lapidary Equipment Co., Sylmar, California.

Fig. 21. A machine shop drill press mounted horizontally to use as a carving arbor. Provisions must be made to protect the motor from grit and debris.

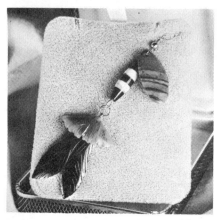

Fig. 23. The body of this fishing lure is made of five pieces of stone, each drilled before the segments were cut from the slice. The pieces were cemented together and then formed and finished as one unit. The lure is made of jade, sardonyx, sagenite, and agate. Photo courtesy of Paul Evans, Caldwell, Idaho.

Some carvings require a lot of drilling, others little or none. See Fig. 23. Bowls, vases, cups, and dishes must be internally drilled or shaped. The suggested procedure is to block out the stone to the desired size and do the drilling before any further work is done on the outside. This provides a flat surface for mounting on the drill press and also a suitable surface for starting the drill or shaping tool. Clamps are used to hold

Fig. 24. Core drills made of steel tubing for abrasive cutting of holes, round cabochons, rings, etc. are available from most lapidary supply stores.

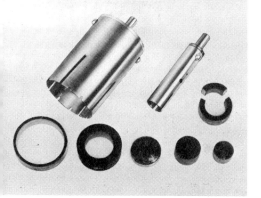

the stone to the base of the drill press.

Wet silicon carbide grit is the cutting agent commonly used. Grit size may vary from 100 to 220 with the larger tools using the larger grit. A shallow well is formed with modeling clay which holds the grit slurry in a confined area. The drills or shaping tools used in the drill press can be of copper, brass, or steel. See Fig. 24

In operation the grit quickly stops cutting unless the tool is raised slightly, allowing more grit to work under the bit. This is usually an automatic operation on a regular gem drill shown in Fig. 25.

The metal tools gradually change shape as they are used. A tube will begin to taper with use and must be reversed or replaced. Tools with a specific shape will need redressing to produce a consistent pattern in internal forming.

Electric Motors

An electric motor should be provided for each unit installed. For the sanding arbor and trim saw, motors of 1/4 hp are sufficient. Used motors are often used for this work.

The slabbing saw requires a larger motor, the power being dependent on the blade size. Again following the manufacturer's advice.

Sources of Supply

With the increase in carving and subsequent demand for development of equipment, no attempt will be made to specify or recommend a certain type of machine. Current information on equipment of this kind can always be obtained through the advertisements in the lapidary and gem magazines. A majority of the rock shops deal in lapidary tools and can be of service in furnishing suitable equipment. If the item you need is not carried in stock, a source of supply can usually be found.

A subscription to one or more of the magazines covering all phases of the rock hobby is also strongly advised. Each issue contains several articles of interest. Leading manufacturers advertise both standard and new items of equipment. Shop helps and special procedures in handling of certain stones are discussed. Hunting areas are described and located, as well as listings of many sources of rocks for sale. A list and review of many rock shows is an interesting feature. No better way can be found to stay in touch with "rock news" than through these magazines.

Carving Cost

One of the foremost questions of many, perhaps, is what will this hobby cost,

It will cost something, of course. Fishing, hunting, golf, or any hobby or craft requires certain tools of the trade. In any case its cost is related to the extent to which we participate.

We may buy a fiishing license, cut a willow for a pole, attach to it a twine string and a bent pin, and go fiishing. The cost? Negative. Fish caught? Likely none. At the other extreme, we may buy excessively of the finest tackle, a boat and trailer, a camper, and invest a great deal of money. We may catch more fish. Certainly, if it is a hobby we like, we would enjoy it more.

The same applies to carving. You can start easily and cheaply or fully equip your shop for any project before you start to work. If you now have conventional lapidary equipment, the additional investment is comparatively small.

In the absence of conventional equipment, there are ways in which to keep the investment down and still do some carving. Slices of stone can be purchased for each special use. Or, if you have rough rock and no saw, you can hire it sawed as desired. Instructions for a carving in the round using only a carving arbor will be found in Chapter 8 (Fig. 75).

Rather than say it costs so many dollars and cents, which varies so much according to how you equip your shop, we advise inquiry at your dealer for your particular needs.

Space for a Workshop

A speciial building to use as a workshop is not a necessity. Part of a basement or garage will serve fine for this purpose. Perhaps a back porch or util-

Fig. 25. An abrasive tube drill set up in a regular drill press for drilling. A grit slurry is held by the modeling clay dam.

ity room can be used. It is seldom the new, clean, and perfectly equipped shop that produces the best lapidary work. Conversely, some of the finest carvings have originated in humble surroundings with insufficient and outdated equipment.

Some things to consider when selecting a work space are the convenience of electrical outlets, the lighting, and the capacity of the wiring circuit to safely handle the load.

Fig. 26. Mandrels. The three on the right are used for discs, wheels and buffs; the two on the left for cone-shaped felts and rubber bonded abrasives. They average about 2 inches long.

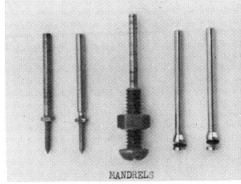

MANDRELS

Chapter 5

Tools and How to Use Them

The equipment described in Chapter 4 is described in the order in which it is normally used. After the 8-inch grinder, the normal procedure is to use the carving arbor and small tools described in this chapter. But in actual operation, a carving seldom leaves one machine never to return. For instance, while using the large grinder it is common to discover a small area that can be more quickly worked with the trimsaw. So back it goes. The same is true from large to small grinding wheels and all through the procedure. If carving was done on a repeat, production line basis, this likely would not happen. But the amateur usually carves one of a kind so each carving is a new experience.

This shifting to a faster tool is encouraged. And since it is common in the shop, some reference to backtracking will occur in the instruction.

Mandrels for Unmounted Accessories

In Fig. 26, are shown some of the small mandrels used with the carving arbor. Most accessories of one inch or less in diameter are used with mandrels of various sizes, with 3/32 and 1/8 inch being commonly used. Collets to fit the different size mandrels are interchangeable in the same chuck. The mandrel is secured in the chuck and the tool to be used is attached to the opposite end.

Several mandrels should be available so that each wheel or disc can be changed as a unit rather than to change the tool on the mandrel. A small screwdriver is the only tool needed for this assembly. The mandrel is tightened in the chuck by hand.

Small Grinding Wheels

Unmounted grinding wheels, (to be used with mandrels) are more economical than mounted ones and are the main workhorses for removing material at this level. They must, of course, be made of silicon carbide just as the larger wheels are. Several reliable brands are being used for gem carving and give good results. We started with the Mizzy Heatless wheels shown in Fig. 27, which have given excellent service on the carving arbor. They range up to one inch in diameter by 1/8-inch or 3/16-inch thick.

In our experience we have found

Fig. 27. Small, unmounted, silicon carbide wheels. Mizzy wheels available from William R. Hall Company, Lindenwold, New Jersey.

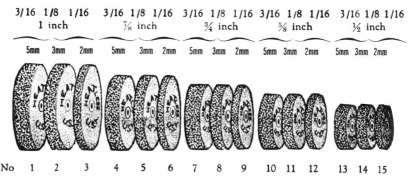

HEATLESS WHEELS

3/16 1/8 1/16	3/16 1/8 1/16	3/16 1/8 1/16	3/16 1/8 1/16	3/16 1/8 1/16
1 inch	⅞ inch	¾ inch	⅝ inch	½ inch
5mm 3mm 2mm	5mm 3mm 2mm	5mm 3mm 2mm	5mm 3mm 2mm	5mm 3mm 2mm
No 1 2 3	4 5 6	7 8 9	10 11 12	13 14 15

SAVE THIS CHART FOR FUTURE REFERENCE

these wheels to be an advantage over using loose grit with a metal tool as a means of grinding or shaping. (Loose grit is used, however, in the sanding operation). Perhaps they are more expensive to use but this is offset by their fast cutting action and convenience. So we suggest the use of the unmounted wheels for the bulk of the grinding. An arbor shaft speed of 5,000 rpm is satisfactory.

Specific jobs will create the need for wheels from one inch down to almost mandrel size. So the thrifty way is buy the one inch diameter as soon you will have a smaller wheel. It can be trued when necessary by holding a piece of discarded grinding wheel to the uneven surface as shown in Fig. 28.

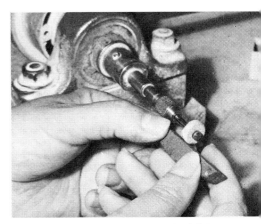

Fig. 28. A small silicon carbide wheel being trued with a piece of discarded grinding wheel. Wheels may also be shaped for special purposes in this way.

While working a carving at this stage, keep a variety of grinding tools handy and change them as the need arises. As an example, a fast cutting grinding wheel will have its corners rounded when used for making a groove. This leaves a U shape at the bottom of the cut. The groove can be cleaned up, if desired, by using a number of separating discs (discussed later in this chapter) mounted together to form a wheel. They will cut slower but leave clean, sharp corners.

Recessed areas in a carving, shown in Fig. 29, can be cut with small wheels by rotating the carving as it is being ground. This forms a round, concave area, or it may become an oval by moving the carving lengthwise. A cupped flower can be formed in this manner.

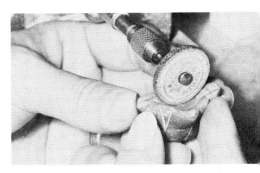

Fig. 29. A recessed, cupped area being ground for a carving of a flower. The wheel stays stationary and the stone is rotated and moved as required.

Fig. 30. Mounted abrasive points. Many sizes and shapes can be obtained.

Grinding wheels of this size can be used wet or dry. It is a good practice, however, to use them wet unless the mud created by the grinding obscures the detail. Wetting is done by dipping a finger into a shallow bowl of water and applied with a light touch to the wheel while it is running. An alternate method is to wet the stone being carved and it in turn wets the grinding wheel.

Applied use of these grinding wheels will be found in Chapters 7, 8 and 9.

Mounted Abrasive Points

Mounted abrasive points of various shapes and sizes can be secured and a selection is needed for detail work.

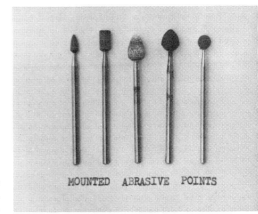

MOUNTED ABRASIVE POINTS

Fig. 31. Three separating discs mounted to cut parallel lines. Small, worn discs are used as spacers.

These points, shown in Fig. 30, may range in size from the point of a lead pencil to a ball or cone 5/16-inch in diameter. They don't remove material very fast, but with a correctly shaped tool for the job, the cutting can be carefully controlled. Mounted points can be used wet or dry and are used with the carving arbor.

This type of tool is used for the eyes and ears in portrait work, or any similar small, recessed area of any carving.

How to Use Separating Discs

The separating disc, sometimes referred to as a cut-off disc, is a thin, silicon carbide disc used extensively in gem carving. The discs can be obtained in different sizes but 7/8 inch in diameter is practical for this craft. A larger size is more easily broken and they get smaller with use which fills the need for smaller discs.

A single disc, or several together as the job requires, is mounted on a mandrel and used with the carving arbor. The separating discs are fragile and can be easily broken, but with proper use they will wear down to the mandrel. They are not worn out as long as their diameter is larger than the diameter of the mandrel. The small ones are often needed for intricate detail work. If the discs wear out-of-round, they can be trued while running with a silicon carbide dresser or a piece of discarded grinding wheel.

Too much pressure or heat will break the discs so don't force or hurry the work. Eliminate heat breakage by wetting the stone as you work. Use the disc dry to cut shallow or small areas of detail which will not create excessive heat. Progress of detail work can be better observed by using the discs dry.

Two or more discs may be mounted together to cut a wider groove. Or, Fig. 31 shows how they may be assembled with a smaller disc between each one as a spacer, thereby cutting parallel lines as they are used.

The straight line is easiest to cut; a sharp curve, the hardest. A small arc requires a small diameter disc. How you hold the stone is very important. As you set at the carving arbor, you will face the cutting edge of the disc mounted in a vertical position. As shown in Figs. 32 and 33, hold the stone under the disc with the marked line pointing toward you and the other end of the line at the disc where the cut is to start. If the curve turns to the right, tip the right edge of the stone up as it travels through its cut. If the curve turns to the left, raise the left side of the stone. It makes the job easier; practice it.

Where there are to be lines, veins,

Fig. 33. Raise the left edge of the stone to make a cut turning to your left.

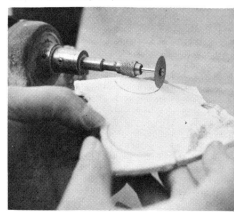

Fig. 32. A separating disc used to make a circular cut. Note the position of the stone.

or detail of any kind cut with these discs, the procedure should follow that of the rough sanding. Better control of the tool is obtained on a rough surface. There is a tendency for the cut to slip sideways as you carve a line and it takes practice to eliminate this problem. You may have better control of the disc by using a slower or a faster speed. Experiment a little with this if you have trouble.

Working on a rough sanded surface is a good practice to follow. If subsequent sandings erase the depth of the markings, they can be recut as necessary before they are erased.

There is no end to the use of this versatile tool. A number of discs can be assembled on a mandrel to form an effective grinding wheel. An advantage of this method is that the thickness of the wheel can be controlled as needed for special cuts.

The discs are effective in forming the detail of the hair, animal fur, fish scales, and many similar details. Specific projects using these discs are discussed in Chapters 7, 8, and 9.

A problem commonly encountered in using small tools, and especially the separating disc, is a tendency at times to force the work. We emphasize "at times." One may go along fine with no thought of passing time, and later the work may be approached in a hurried, forceful, manner. It may be a mood, but whatever the cause, it doesn't work. It breaks small tools and the carving may be damaged.

If the hurried approach can't be eliminated by conscious effort, it's best to leave the work for a later time.

Diamond Tools

Diamond cutting tools are being used more and more by the hobbyist to replace silicon carbide. They include diamond charged drills, saws, mounted points and discs, and diamond sanding cloth. They require a greater outlay of cash, of course, but they also reduce the work time of most operations.

There are other reasons for their use in carving, however. They leave a clean sharp cut and are available in extremely small sizes and a wide variety of shapes.

Fig. 34. A 30x40 mm cameo.

A hard stone, such as sapphire, can be cut only with diamond tools. The advantage of their use is apparent where extremely small detail is required. For carvings such as cameos, shown in Fig. 34, the use of diamond tools is almost mandatory.

Small diamond accessories to be used with the carving arbor are always used with a coolant to prevent heat damage to the tool and stone.

Sanding with Small Tools

Problems are usually encountered in the sanding of a carving. The principle problem is the uneven areas that must be sanded with small tools without destroying the detail or character of the carving. For this reason, the sanding calls for more improvising of methods than any part of the work.

The first suggestion is to use a conventional belt or drum sander on any areas of a carving that permit its use. This practice is limited, by the irregular shape of many subjects so small tools, used in the carving arbor, are next in line.

A supply of small rubber bonded sanding cones and wheels is standard equipment. These are frequently sold in an assortment of sizes and shapes. Grit sizes needed are coarse, medium, fine, and extra fine. These tools, some of which are shown in Fig. 35, are assembled to a suitable mandrel and used, wet or dry, on the carving arbor.

Also shown in Fig. 35 is a drum sander, ¾-inch in diameter, which fills a

25

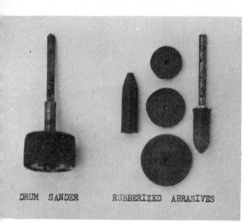

DRUM SANDER   RUBBERIZED ABRASIVES

Fig. 35. Some small tools used for sanding and carving.

need in some areas. The sanding belt is secured in place by tightening a screw which expands the drum. This device works well on relatively smooth areas only. It will destroy fine detail of uneven surfaces.

Small circular discs cut from regular sanding cloth are also useful. Placing two of these, smooth side together, on a mandrel provides a good working tool. They may vary in size depending on the need. A 1-inch grinding wheel makes a good template for marking the outline and center hole for discs of this size.

Hand sanding is not an unusual practice in our shop. It isn't fast, but some conditions require its use. Sanding cloth is cut into triangular pieces and used

Fig. 36. Small wheels cut from ¼-inch, flat, rubberized belting. They are used with loose grits; make good sanding tools.

to get into otherwise inaccessible areas. Don't overlook the possibilities of this method. It frequently solves a difficult sanding problem.

Wheels, up to one inch in diameter, cut from ¼-inch, flat, rubberized belting and mounted on a mandrel have proven quite successful when used with wet grit. See Fig. 36. They make a firm wheel, have a texture coarse enough to hold the grit well, and still will conform to irregular surfaces where fine detail must be preserved. A different wheel, of course, must be used for each grit size.

A hole saw, available at hardware stores, is used in a drill press to cut the wheels from a piece of belting. This operation is shown in Fig. 37. Location for the center hole can be obtained by using a disc or grinding wheel as a template. Use a number 50 drill bit for the center hole.

The periphery of the wheel may be rough as it comes from the hole saw. If so, secure it to a mandrel on the carving arbor and hold a rough file or rasp to the wheel as it turns at slow speed. When properly smoothed it is ready for use.

A slurry of grit and water used with a flat surfaced hand tool, such as the end of a screwdriver, will sand in sharp, offset, right angle corners. The tool is used in a back and forward motion

Fig. 37. A cabinetmaker's hole saw can be used to cut wheels from rubberized belt. A small hole must be drilled in the center for mounting on a mandrel.

with different grits until a proper finish is obtained. Any wheel or cone will round corners and still leave a small area of the corner unsanded.

When using rubber bonded sanding tools on agate, jasper, and perhaps other materials, a glaze will sometimes appear before the surface is really sanded smooth. To correct this, use a coarser grit tool to start the operation. Then change in successive steps to finer grit to get the right finish. Using the tools wet will sometimes get results not otherwise attainable. Water is applied with a finger as work progresses.

The arbor shaft speed for sanding may vary somewhat with the tool being used. In general, shaft speeds of 2500 to 5000 rpm are used with good results.

In any sanding operation, a change to a finer grit requires careful washing of the hands, the carving, and other areas where the coarser grit may be lodged. Pay special attention with a carving in cleaning recessed areas or grooves that may not wash out freely. Cleaning is necessary to prevent scratches which are caused by the coarser grit carrying into the next operation.

Polishing

If the carving is properly sanded, the polishing is no problem. Conventional polishing equipment is more effective than small tools so use it whenever possible. A 6-inch muslin buff will conform quite well to the irregular surface of a carving. See Fig. 38.

When small tools are required, they are only miniatures of the larger ones, i.e. leather, muslin, or felt wheels or cones. Felt wheels used for polishing are shown in Fig. 39.

These tools are assembled to a mandrel and used with the carving arbor. The arbor speed must be somewhat slower than used for grinding and sanding to prevent the polish from being thrown from the tool. Polish may, however, be applied to the stone which allows a faster speed when necessary.

Several different polishing agents are available. The selection is determined both by personal opinion and the stone to be polished. Commonly used are tin

Fig. 38. A 6-inch muslin buff being used to polish a carving. The surface of a muslin buff conforms more easily to irregular surfaces than leather or hard felt.

oxide, aluminum oxide, chromium oxide, cerium oxide and Linde A.

Chromium oxide has been a standard polish for jade for many years. Other agents also used extensively are tin oxide and Linde A. Where conditions permit, the use of leather for polishing jade is highly recommended.

The polishing agents are all used with water to form a creamy consistency. A small amount is applied to the wheel or tool being used as polishing continues.

Small Hand Held Tools

Only a few special hand tools are necessary. A 6-inch scale or ruler with fine graduation is very useful. A divider is needed at times for the making

Fig. 39. Small felt buffs, mounted on a mandrel, are often used for polishing.

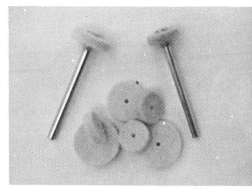

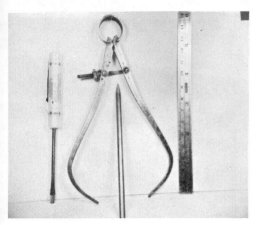

Fig. 40. Tools for taking and transferring accurate measurements are about all that are necessary in hand tools.

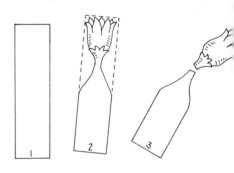

Fig. 41. A practical method for carving very small parts. Start with enough stone for both the piece and a handle. Shape, sand and polish completely and then carefully cut the carving from the handle.

and transferring of measurements. See Fig. 40.

Several aluminum pencils will be needed. These may be purchased or made from aluminum wire sharpened to a point.

A magnifying glass is needed quite often for close inspection of a stone as well as to observe the quality of workmanship. The type which can be worn on the head in the manner of a visor is very handy. It can be brought into use by tilting the head slightly forward and can be used with regular glasses.

Dust Control

Water should be used whenever possible both to cool the stone and to keep dust to a minimum. Fine detail, however, is often hard to see when the work is wet, so this type of carving must be done dry. Unfortunately, particles from the stone and the wearing away of silicon carbide tools can be very hazardous to the health, so the use of a vacuum cleaner or some other type of dust removal equipment is strongly recommended. It is also a good idea to wear an approved dust mask or respirator.

Dop Sticks

A dop stick is a handle. It is assembled to a small preformed stone to assist in the handling of the grinding and subsequent operations. Ordinary nails may be used or the sticks may be cut from wooden dowel of different sizes. Dopping wax, available at rock shops, is used to hold the stone to the dop stick. Application is made by dipping the end of the dop stick into the melted wax and applying it to the stone, which must also be warmed.

This is standard practice and works well for cabochons. Handling small carvings this way is somewhat limited because of their shape. A small carving may have to be manipulated so many ways while grinding and sanding that the dop stick gets in the way rather than helps. If so, the object must be held in the hands while carrying out the various operations.

A method which works well for extremely small parts is quite simple. Rather than to use a dop stick, we have found it practical to start with enough stone to form the carving plus length enough to use as a handle on the same piece of stone. Fig. 41 shows a small flower which is easily ground, sanded, and polished before the handle is cut off. The small connecting area (where the flower is cut off) is then finished by holding the carving in the hand.

Chapter 6

Carving Forms and Finishes

To prevent a hit and miss plan of action, we must consider carving forms, color, and finish in connection with the stone to be used. The plan and the stone must be compatible for a carving to be successful.

Carving Forms

Two terms comonly used among rock hobbyists to classify gem carving as to form are *flat work* and *carvings in the round.* "In the round," of course, means that the carving has three dimensions — height, width, and depth — all being maintained in their natural, relative proportion.

A carving developed from a relatively thin section is called *flat work.* Height and width are maintained naturally but depth is reduced. The object — and the problem — is to create the effect of depth with a relatively thin slice of stone. See Fig. 42.

In addition to these forms, there is one widely used in oriental carvings. To our knowledge, it is seldom employed in the United States. These are *relief carvings.* They may be further classified as *high or low relief,* which are simply comparative indications of depth of the designs. In other words, a carving is "relieved" to the extent the designs or figures stand out from the background.

Many oriental carvings, cut in three dimensions, are further decorated with relief carvings of many designs.

A relief design may be carved into the side of a rough, uncut stone with good results. We recently had the pleasure of seeing a fine example of this type in competition at one of the rock shows.

A combination of low and high relief is sometimes used in the same carving. Here the different cuts are used to attain the illusion of distance or depth, as in a landscape scene. High relief is used in the foreground which is diminished at different planes, as necessary, to low relief in the distance.

The successful use of relief carvings, as in flat work, depends upon the ability to create the effect of depth while width and heighth are maintained naturally.

A carving need not be thick or round to be classed as three dimensional. If it conforms to the natural subject from which it is patterned, then it has its third dimension. The leaf shown in Fig. 43 is one example. Although it is flat as compared to a thicker subject, it has its natural form. Flat work is

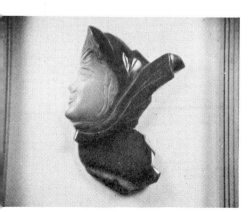

Fig. 42. A portrait carved from a ¼-inch slice of Bruneau jasper. It creates the illusion of depth from a thin stone.

Fig. 43. A leaf, 2 inches long, carved from green jade.

Fig. 44. This carving, considered flat work, is cut from a ¼ x 3-inch slice of chert. We call him the "Scientist."

considered to be modified from the round or natural to one reduced in thickness, as shown in Fig. 44.

Round or Flat

The mechanics involved in the two types of carvings vary considerably. There can be no definite statement as to which is the most difficult to achieve because several factors are involved. The material used, the design and form of the object, available tools necessary, and even the experience of the carver in certain areas all have a bearing on which type may require the most skill.

Generally speaking, the three dimensional carving usually requires that more material be removed. To achieve the correct proportion and shape from all sides may be perplexing as the work progresses. More time is usually involved in this type of carving, especially if finished in detail.

Flat work is usually carved from a slice of stone or a conveniently shaped thin stone in its original form. Quite often this type of carving is done in great detail.

Show Action

It's advisable and more enjoyable to create your own design rather than to copy another's. This doesn't imply that you must not carve an elephant because an elephant has been carved by another. But, use your own style. Project your own ideas in your work. A carving

comes to life when it tells a story or shows action. See Fig. 45. It may be designed to deliver a message. Work of this nature tends to add character and interest to a gem carving.

Don't Leave It Blocky

Unless a craving is started from a stone in its natural shape, it is of necessity first a slice, square, or, perhaps, a rectangular block of stone. One must guard against the common tendency to finish the item with this original shape still discernible. Although the corners may be ground and shaped and detail cut, the experienced carver can detect a lack of work in this area. This is not an intentional oversight by the craftsman, but it is sometimes overlooked unless brought to his attention.

Features Without Color

In most gemstone carvings we don't have the use of colors to obtain the effect or depth and clarity of detail as in a drawing or painting. Many subjects are carved from a single-colored material. Contrast is obtained, then, only by the use of the stone itself rather than by color. Detail is achieved and controlled by the depth and sharpness of a cut to produce a shadow. The surface

Fig. 45. A bird of honey onyx (calcite), a carving in the round. The wingspread is 4 ½ inches. The obsidian eye was formed by the method shown in Fig. 41. It was inset by drilling with a dental burr on the carving arbor.

texture, or texture of the finish, plays an important part in the appearance of the completed work. Tone, a change from light to dark, can be achieved by texture of finish on many materials.

Polish vs. Appropriate Finish

At times it is difficult to determine whether a carving or parts of a carving should have a high polish until it has been tried. It is not unusual to remove a polish to a more suitable finish when it detracts from a carving's effectiveness. A general rule of the thumb is to follow nature. If in nature it shines, polish it. If it has a soft finish, duplicate it.

Vases or bowls may be made of colorful material and look well with a high polish. Some animals carved in stone look excellent with most of the area highly polished. A leaf in one material may look well polished and in another may have a harsh, unnatural appearance. The human figure requires different finishes. The face and hands require a soft finish, clothing may be polished, and the hair polished or high lighted. A mask can accept a polish where a face in detail must vary in finish. Polish, or lack of it, is much more important in some types of carving than others.

In this respect we are interested in results, not custom. If a high polish produces the finish you want, use it. If not, experiment until you feel you have done your best for that particular piece of work.

After all, who can better judge what constitutes a proper finish than the one who designs and executes a carving? The emphasis here is on "proper finish" and may or may not include a high polish. The fact that a high polish brings out the natural beauty of a stone does not always mean that it enhances a carving, even though it is made of stone.

Opinions differ. One who works only in the phases of lapidary where an excellent polish is the prime objective, may view carvings with this basis of comparison. A carver's own style and the objects he likes best to do may influence some instances. Many times different finishes on the same carving are required. *A finish which best suits the subject should be the objective.*

The Little Drummer Boy by Dr. Charles Irvin, DVM, Yucaipa, California. The cherub was carved from a block of Tick Canyon howlite.

Chapter 7

So far we've looked at gem carving from a distance. We've discussed gem materials and equipment. We've looked for sources of ideas and studied carving forms, color, and finishes. Now let's make a start by applying these ideas to a stone.

Printed instructions always seem long and complicated, whether they instruct in carving a stone or making a pie. But the instructions always become amazingly simple after the work is once completed. It is good, then, to keep this in mind as you study this procedure. With a little experience, some of the steps can be done almost as quickly as reading about them.

Fig. 46. You can use this drawing of a leaf to reproduce a pattern for the carving steps to follow.

1. In Figs. 46 to 58 we have shown the steps in carving a leaf. Start by making a pattern over the drawing in Fig. 46 by using tracing paper. If the pattern is to be reused several times, it should be transferred to a durable material and cut out as a template. Otherwise, the image may be transferred from the tracing paper to the stone by a carbon paper. Retrace the lines with an aluminum pencil.

The slice of stone should be approximately 3/16-inch thick. After the leaf is drawn in detail, draw straight lines surrounding the leaf as shown in Fig. 47. This is necessary only for your first few carvings. After that the lines become imaginary and need not be drawn.

2. Using the trim saw, cut out the leaf by sawing to the lines as shown in Fig. 48. Instructions for using the trim saw is given in Chapter 4. Leave a margin of about 1/16-inch between the pattern and the saw cut. This practice also can be eliminated later, but for the beginner it leaves a margin for error in sawing and a narrow margin for grinding to the contour of the pattern.

Continue sawing until the leaf is blocked out in straight cuts.

3. Shape the edges of the leaf by grinding to the marked outline as indi-

Fig. 47. Transfer the pattern with carbon paper and redraw the lines with an aluminum pencil. Enclose the leaf in straight lines as a guide for sawing.

Fig. 48. Three saw cuts made. Saw to the straight lines but be careful not to saw into the pattern.

cated in Fig. 49. This may be done on an 8-inch grinding wheel, using the corners of the wheel when necessary. Grind to a 90 degree angle from the face of the stone, just as it was sawed. Hold the stone firmly with two hands as you apply light pressure to the wheel.

4. Grind a groove lengthwise in the leaf, as shown in Fig. 50, by holding the stone to the corner of the grinding wheel. Make the cut deeper at each end of the leaf than at the center, leaving a curve from the center to each end. This becomes the location for the center vein of the leaf. Figure 51 shows how the leaf is held to the grinding wheel.

5. The vein locations to the edge of the leaf are ground in the same manner. Redraw if necessary and notice the direction and location of each vein. Grind each one from the edge to the center vein, curved down at the edge, sloping up to the center. Leave pronounced ridges between the veins as they are ground. Continue until all grooves are complete on the front of the leaf, shown in Fig. 52.

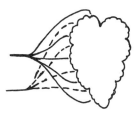

Fig. 53. Grind grooves on the back side of the leaf as indicated in this drawing.

Turn the leaf over and grind grooves as indicated in Fig. 53. These are placed between the grooves on the front of the leaf. Taper these grooves out at the center. There is no lengthwise groove on the back of the leaf. When this grinding is complete, there should be no blunt areas at the edges or ends. If there is, regrind the tapered end of the grooves to form a relatively thin edge. This is an important feature. The finish at the edges can make a leaf look thin and delicate. or, if improperly done, will leave it thick and blocky. The edge should appear as shown in Fig. 54.

6. The entire sanding procedure on this leaf may be done on an 8-inch drum

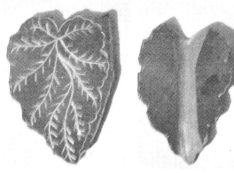

Fig. 49. Grind the outline, as shown on the left side in the picture, with a 6- or 8-inch grinding wheel.

Fig. 50. Grind a groove from top to bottom of the leaf using the grinding wheel.

Fig. 51. The groove for the center vein of the leaf is being ground here. When using the corner of a grinding wheel, stand at the corner, not in front of the wheel.

Fig. 52. Continue by grinding grooves as shown on the left side of the leaf. The drawn veins indicate the position of the grooves.

Fig. 54. The edge of the leaf as it should appear after the grooves are ground on both the front and back.

33

Fig. 55. This picture shows the leaf with the grooves completed and the rough sanding finished with 220 grit cloth.

Fig. 56. This shows the veins marked as they are to be cut with a small separating disc.

Fig. 57. A separating disc is also used to serrate the edges of the leaf.

Fig. 58. The leaf as it appears after final sanding and polishing.

sander or a belt sander. The edge of the sanding cloth will conform somewhat to the shape of the grooves to be sanded. First use a 220-grit cloth and sand each individual groove. Both edges of the sander can be used, and the leaf must be turned many times to complete each contour of every groove.

This step completes the shaping of the leaf and should eliminate grinding marks or irregularities. Figure 55 shows the appearance of the leaf at this stage of completion.

7. Figure 56 shows the veins marked with an aluminum pencil, just as they are to be carved. Assemble a mandrel and a separating disc to the carving arbor for this operation. How to use the separating disc is explained in Chapter 5.

Proceed to cut the veins as they are marked in Fig. 57. There is sanding yet to do, so cut deep enough to leave a distinct line. The disc must be small to cut the short lines that project from each vein. Cut them at an angle to the vein to prevent the disc from cutting into the edges of the grooves.

Use the separating discs also to serrate the edges of the leaf. These need not be uniformly spaced; strive to give the leaf a natural appearance.

8. Wash the leaf thoroughly to remove all grit. A small brush is used to clean the veins and recessed areas. Now sand on the 8-inch drum sander using 400-grit cloth. Rewash and repeat sanding with 600-grit cloth. Wash again.

9. Polish the leaf on a 6- or 8-inch muslin buff which will conform to the irregular shape of the leaf. Hold the stone firmly in both hands as there is danger of it being pulled from your hands. Figure 58 shows the finished leaf.

How Green Is Your Thumb?

Following these instructions will produce a carved leaf, even though it may lack some of the character you'd like it to have. The old adage that we must learn to walk before we can learn to run fits well here. Some trial and error is common rather than unusual.

Your first leaf may appear as a stone carved into a leaf. Your objective should be to make it appear as a leaf turned to stone.

Chapter 8

Carving in The Round

Three different carvings are described in this chapter. Each one is a carving in the round but work methods make each a different kind of carving with its own advantages or problems. Number 1 instructs in the ordinary procedure of most carvings in the round. Number 2 shows an example where no mass of material need be removed. Number 3 requires a drilling operation in connection with a carving in the round.

It isn't to be inferred that only three variations of three dimensional carvings exist. But in pointing out these differences, basic instruction can be applied to many of the forms commonly used for a carving. Select your design and fit the instruction to it.

MOTHER AND BABE
Using a Model

Let's follow through the procedure for a carving in the round where a lot of material is to be removed. We'll use as our objective the *Mother and Babe*, a carving which was first envisioned and modeled with clay. It started from "scratch" with no picture, ceramic, or other model to follow. It started with an idea and a chunk of clay. Two hundred and forty carving hours later the Mother was holding her Babe as shown in Fig. 59. The instructions here are what happened during those hours.

A scale of size was first determined to fit the stone which was to be used for the carving. Modeling (with children's modeling clay) was done in some detail to get a clearer picture of what we were working toward. Measurements were then taken from the completed model, shown in Fig. 60, and transferred to the stone to be used. From these measurements a suitable rectangular block was marked and cut out with the slabbing saw.

A rough image was then drawn on the side and also on the face of the block. The drawings, Figs. 61 and 62, show a large amount of stone to be removed. This is not unusual but about par for many carvings in the round.

Grinding is a slow way to remove material so the answer is to use the diamond saw wherever possible. The problem is how to get the job done the easiest and fastest way.

Preform with the Saw

The saw cuts represented in Figs. 61 and 62 were made by securing the rectangular rock in a temporary, vertical, extension of the vise. This method of sawing, which may be used on many

Fig. 59. Light pink agate was used to carve this 5½-inch Mother and Babe. The chair is petrified wood.

Fig. 60. Measurements for the carving were taken from this modelling clay model.

35

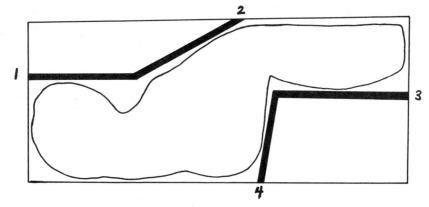

Fig. 61. A side view of the drawing on a block of stone. Saw cuts 1 through 4 show the large areas of stone to be removed by sawing.

carvings, is described in Chapter 4, Figs. 7, 8, and 9. By changing the position of the rock in the vise, as required, the bulk of the material was sawed away.

Here's some advice: Don't skimp on any cut that can be made with the saw; it's more efficient than other methods.

Shaping with the Saw

Although the bulk of the material was cut away with the slabbing saw, each sawed surface left a flat, blocky, square cornered, preform of a carving. The trim saw was used to tackle the problem of rounding these flats and corners.

Important things to remember: A deep cut may be made *only if the carv-*

Fig. 62. The front view of the drawing on the stone shows additional cuts which were made by using the vise extension shown in Fig. 7.

ing is positioned or held solidly on the trim saw table. If hand-held, material is removed by making shallow, parallel or crisscross, cuts. Don't make a cut deep. Visualize the saw blade as a grinding wheel for this phase of the work.

The carving was turned to many angles on all sides as it was preshaped with this tool. Sharp corners were removed with short parallel cuts of the right depth. Material below each arm was removed by cuts parallel to the arm with the carving positioned on its back. As each cut was made, some part of the stone remained on the saw table as a support. The depth of the cut was controlled by slowly turning the top of the stone into the saw as the desired depth at the bottom was reached. This procedure is shown in Fig. 63 and 64. In effect, this changes the point of contact of the saw with the stone. When a cut is started, it cuts first *at the table top.* To prevent sawing too deeply at

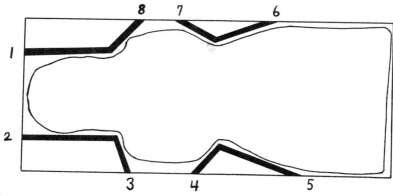

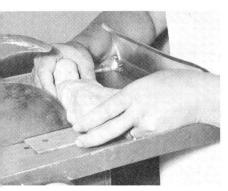
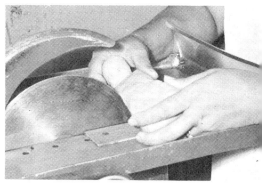

Fig. 63. Additional material is removed with a trim saw. Sometimes the splash guard must be propped up to allow more working room.

Fig. 64. Note the difference in the position of the stone here as compared to Fig. 63. Here the stone is held at a different angle to the blade. The part of the stone resting on the table is pulled away slightly from the blade as the top of the stone is fed into the blade. A fairly even cut from top to bottom can be obtained this way.

the table top, "roll" the stone into the blade which changes the point of contact. Depending on its shape, a wedge may be required beneath the back edge of the stone to properly support it.

Material was removed from other parts of the carving in a similar way. Figure 65 shows the carving after some work was done with the trim saw and then smoothed with a large grinder.

Shaping with a Large Grinder

This is a difficult stage of a carving in the round. It is not so much how-to as where-to. The lines are obliterated. It's too rough and undeveloped as yet to redraw the image. Such was the condition of the Mother and Babe as work was completed with the trim saw. It was a jagged, rough, ill-shaped piece of rock.

The 8-inch grinder was used now to smooth the rough areas as shown in Fig. 66. This operation, too, required grinding in many areas from many angles. The carving was turned to different positions and alternately ground on each corner of the wheel for the hard to reach places. The model was studied often and the carving uniformly developed.

When the surface was again relatively smooth, the carving form began to reappear for the first time since the first sawing destroyed the original drawing.

Redraw the Image

Work was stopped at this time and measurements from the clay model were marked on the stone. The top and bot-

Fig. 65. The carving at an early stage, after using the slab saw, the trim saw, and some smoothing with a large grinding wheel.

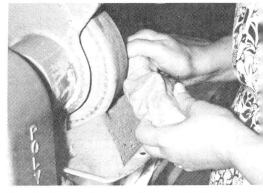

Fig. 66. The grinder is used to smooth the rough areas left by the trim saw and to further develop the carving's form.

Fig. 67. Grind with 1-inch wheels where the size of the area permits.

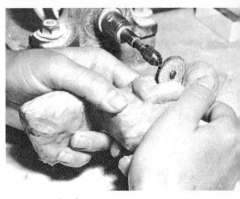

Fig. 68. Develop the carving uniformly by grinding in all areas.

tom (head and foot) of the carving were correct at this stage because no extra stone was allowed when the rectangle was sawed. So measurements were marked from the top of the head to the shoulder, from the shoulder to the elbow, from the elbow to the cuff of the sleeve. The width of the skirt was marked at different points and the position of the Babe was established. Lines were then drawn to connect these points of measurement and again we had an outlined drawing of the image.

The drawing showed material that must still be removed. If the area justified and/or permitted the use of the trim saw, it again was used and the roughened area resmoothed with the grinder. Other areas developed with the grinder at this time were the shape of the head and hair, the back, below the arms, the hips, and the shoulders. The bust, face, and neck were yet to be formed and no clear outline of the draping blanket was yet established. These required the use of the carving arbor and small tools.

A problem commonly experienced in carvings in the round is to start the detail work too soon. The form may not be ground to correct size, or part of it may be out of proportion. This causes extra work (with the detail) for the area must still be ground away. Carving experience helps, of course, but in addition: 1. Be conscious of this problem as detail work is contemplated, 2. Com-

pare measurements carefully with the model and the carving.

Shaping with Small Tools

Any lines which were ground away were now redrawn. This is the best self-starter there is when the thing looks impossible. It helps to establish a mental image of the carving.

A single separating disc was used on the carving arbor to outline the hair at the forehead, neck, and shoulders. The material at the upper portion of the body was removed, primarily with unmounted wheels of various sizes. See Figs. 67 and 68. The 1-inch wheels were used first and as areas became restricted in size, smaller wheels were used. The deep, recessed area between the body and the arms was made with a grinding wheel. Small wheels and discs were used in shaping the face and neck.

Some of the area under the jaw, at the hairline, presented a problem common to many carvings. The diameter

Fig. 69. A cone-shaped, silicon carbide tool is being used in a restricted area.

of the area required a wheel or disc so small that the mandrel hit the adjacent stone before the desired depth was reached. This was solved by using mounted abrasive points of suitable shapes, shown in Fig. 69. Cone-shape and ball-shape tools were used for this particular job. Diamond tools also work fine for these areas and are faster than silicon carbide points.

Much of the detail of the face, hands, and hair, shown in Fig. 70, was done with small discs and tiny abrasive points. Carbide steel denture burrs were used for the pupils and corners of the eyes, shown in Fig. 71. These tiny tools, second hand from a dentist friend, don't last long but in the absence of diamond points of suitable size, they will do a small amount of work on soft stone. To buy them new for use on agate, jade, etc., would not be practical. But if you have access to these discarded burrs, you'll find some use for them. Only the carbide steel burrs are effective; the ordinary steel burrs are useless for this work.

Other areas developed with wheels and discs were the Babe and the folds of the blanket.

The nicks and cuts made during the shaping of the carving were now smoothed with the same shaping tools. They're more efficient for the initial smoothing of a chopped-up surface than the small sanders.

Sanding the Carving

The entire surface of this carving was sanded with small tools. One area of the dress and blanket was large enough for an 8-inch drum sander, but it would only flatten the folds of the dress and thus destroy the detail.

The coarse sanding must be thorough. Actually, it's an inbetween step. It completes the shaping and starts the sanding.

A ¾-inch drum sander, shown in Fig. 72, was first used in all the easy to reach places. Sanding on the clothing and blanket was done parallel to the folds. If deep recesses were not reached, rubber bonded cones or discs were used on the same area later to correct this.

Much of the upper part of the body,

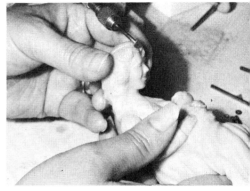

Fig. 70. Details of the hair being developed with a ¼-inch diamond disc.

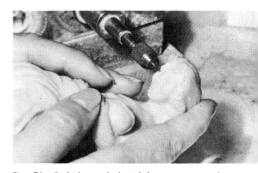

Fig. 71. Carbide steel dental burrs were used for the pupils and corners of the eyes. They dull rapidly and should be used only when no other tool will do.

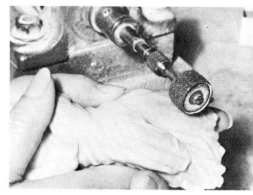

Fig. 72. A ¾-inch drum sander was used in easy-to-reach places. Rubber bonded abrasive cones and discs were also used extensively.

the neck, and other hard to reach places were sanded with rubber bonded abrasives. Cone shapes seemed to work best here. A felt wheel and grit was used on the hands and similar areas

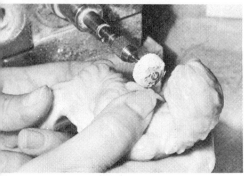

Fig. 73. Polishing was done with a muslin buff using tin oxide as a polishing agent.

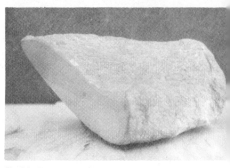

Fig. 74. A piece of light green variscite in the rough. The dealer had polished one end to show the color and quality.

where detail would be easily erased. In other areas, wheels made from belting were used with grit.

The sanding operation was carried through to the fine grit except on the blanket. It was sanded with 400 grit and received no additional finishing. This produced a soft, textured, natural appearance that set it apart from the polished dress. To obtain this finish, use a wet, grit slurry, rather than sanding cloth.

The sanding operation took, perhaps, about one-third of the time required for the entire carving.

Polish

Fig. 73 shows how the carving was polished with felt cones and felt or muslin buffs used on the carving arbor. Two problems encountered in polishing are caused by improper sanding of the stone, or, a poor quality stone. The stone should be checked before the carv-

ing is started and a more thorough sanding job solves the other problem. Otherwise, the polishing is relatively simple and fast compared to the other phases of the work.

THE SPICE MERCHANT

There are a lot of possibilities for carving stones in their natural form, just as they are found. To do so, the form of the stone must be studied and a plan drawn to fit the stone.

While this presents a challenge, other aspects of this method have distinct advantages. The operation can be done without using a slabbing saw, a trim saw, or a large grinder. To the mobile home craftsman this can present opportunities for carving in the round that conventional methods prohibit for the carving arbor and accessories take little space.

A disadvantage is the inability to always determine if the stone is fracture free. Also, the work range is narrowed, but it is a way to start with little investment or to meet problems of restricted space.

Figs. 74 and 75 show a carving which was designed to use the stone in its original size and form. This saved a lot of time in the initial stages of the carving. The stone is gray green variscite, free of pattern.

Fig. 75. This gentleman, the spice merchant, was carved from the piece of variscite shown in Fig. 74. No material was removed except to create the detail of the form. The base is walnut.

The plan for the carving took time and experimenting before a suitable design was made. The first drawings on the stone were made with pencil so erasure was easy. When the drawing was finally right, it was redrawn with an aluminum pencil. Then the outline was established by making a shallow cut along the lines with a separating disc.

The work on this carving was done entirely with the carving arbor and an assortment of small tools. The grinding was started on the folds of the headdress with a 1-inch wheel. The same tool was used to make the deep recess at each side of the face and to form the neck. The face was left untouched at this time.

Additional shaping and smoothing of the inside of the headdress, which drapes around the face and neck, was done with mounted points of various shapes.

The facial features were redrawn on the stone, where necessary, and work was started with a small diameter wheel. The nose emerged by removing material from below and at each side. A suitable area was ground for each eye. The lips were formed with small separating discs and wheels and the chin and cheeks were the last to be formed.

No part of the face was completed before another was started. Each area was only preformed and both sides of the face were developed together. Each area was repeatedly reworked until the parts became a face.

The wrinkles in the forehead and face were formed by making deep cuts with a disc. The cuts were then smoothed with a sharp-edged rubber bonded wheel. Round, mounted points formed the pupils of the eyes.

Rubber bonded abrasives worked well on this material and were used extensively for the sanding. Polishing was done with small muslin wheels on the carving arbor.

JADE VASE

The material for this carving, shown in Fig. 76, was bought as a rectangular, sawed block and the vase was designed to take full advantage of its height and width.

Fig. 76. A 3½-inch vase carved from green jade. The hole was drilled first and then the exterior was sawed and ground to form.

The drilling operation, first to be completed, was done before any outside material was removed. Two diagonal lines were drawn from opposite corners on one end of the block to locate the center for drilling. With this as a guide, the size and position of the hole was marked.

Drilling a Carving

A steel tube drill, 5/8-inch in diameter, was first secured in the drill press. The rectangular block of jade was then placed in position and held by two clamps. Modeling clay was used to form a reservoir around the tube, in which a slurry of 180 grit silicon carbide and water was placed.

The drill press was set to run at about 2500 rpm and drilling was started by gently lowering the tube to the stone. After the cutting was started, the gem drill automatically raised and lowered the tube which allowed grit to flow to the cutting edge. A slurry of grit was frequently added to the reservoir. The cutting action is observed by the sound; if the grit runs low, the sound is less grating and quieter.

No time was recorded for the drilling of this vase but it is a slow operation. The hole was drilled to a depth of about 2 inches. The block was then removed from the drill press and the core removed by wedging a small tool beside it. This can be safely done only when the surrounding area is stronger than the core.

41

Fig. 77. Sanding was done with 220-, 400-, and 600-grit cloth.

Fig. 78. The vase was turned forward and back to prevent sanding flat spots. This must be done on any round or curved surface when using a drum sander.

Fig. 79. Polishing with leather and cerium oxide was done on the carving arbor.

A drawing of the vase was next made on two sides of the sawed block. The slabbing saw with the vise extension, explained in Chapter 4, was used to remove excess material. The upper part of the vase was sawed out first, then the corners of the block were sawed from the bottom part of the vase.

The shaping was completed with a large grinder. The shape of the carving presented no problem so sanding was done with 220-, 300-, and 600-grit cloth on a drum sander, as shown in Figs. 77 and 78.

Polishing the carving, shown in Fig. 79, was done on a leather wheel using chromium oxide as a polishing agent. The leather wheel was used on the carving arbor at the opposite end from the chuck.

Chapter 9

Portraits in Stone

Perhaps the greatest challenge in gem carving is to create a likeness of a person's face. A close second to this is to create a face portraying emotion, character, or nationality. Just as it is exacting work, it is comparably rewarding to the artisan.

The portrait illustrated in this chapter, as well as many in our collection, is about three inches high. We decided on this scale of size for several reasons. We wanted them larger than cameos so they could be easily viewed in a display case but still of a size that could be cut from an average slice of stone. The face is large enough, also, to receive a lot of revealing character.

It is impractical to work this size portrait with layered material, as you would a cameo with a contrasting background. But stone with layers or color variations can be used with success to distinguish the face from the hair or clothing. To use a stone with a color pattern, the portrait must be drawn to fit the stone.

Figure 80 shows a finished carving of this kind. This seems to come easily for some people and is very difficult for others.

This chapter is devoted to a series of instructions based on a portrait we

Fig. 80. The tan and brown oval patterns, so prominent in Bruneau jasper, were used for this portrait. The design was made to fit the pattern of the stone.

carved. The objective was to create a likeness of Will Rogers. However, the instructions could be used for any similar reproduction.

Fig. 81. This official photograph of Will Rogers was selected as the design and photographic prints made to the exact size needed for the carving.

Fig. 82. Trace the major lines of the image onto tracing paper. Keep the lines sharp.

1. It is important to study several poses of the subject to be carved to better acquaint yourself with the important features. Then select the picture to be used and have a print made to the exact size you want for the carving. Figure 81 shows the picture we selected for this portrait.

2. With the use of a clipboard, secure tracing paper over the picture and transfer the image by tracing all the important lines as shown in Fig. 82. Use a No. 3 or No. 4 pencil to keep all the lines sharp.

For a portrait of this size the slice of stone should be ¼-inch thick. This carving is considered as flat work and the objective is to create the effect of the third dimension, depth, as well as to create a likeness.

3. Now transfer the image from the tracing paper to the stone with the use of carbon paper. Next remove the tracing paper and carbon paper and retrace all the lines with an aluminum pencil. Figure 83 shows the image drawn on the

43

Fig. 85. The image has been sawed out, the edges ground, and the head and shoulders bevelled to the correct angles.

Fig. 83. Transer the lines to the stone with carbon paper; retrace with an aluminum pencil.

Fig. 84. Saw to the outline of the image, as shown here.

Fig. 86. The carving gets more difficult now. Keep important lines, such as the mouth, nose and eyes visible by recutting, as required, with a separating disc.

stone ready to start work.

If you are to make a likeness, each of these steps in drawing contribute to your knowledge of the subject. You may want to create an image of your own design, however, and this can be drawn directly on the stone.

4. Now saw to the outline of the image with the trim saw as shown in Fig. 84. In areas that can't be removed by straight line sawing, make a series of short parallel cuts and break out the remaining stone. Note this — the back side of the slice becomes the outline of the finished carving. Do not saw or grind beyond the marked outline.

5. Smooth the sawed edges on an 8-inch grinding wheel. Grind to the outline at a 90-degree angle to the face of the stone.

Now bevel and shape the head and shoulders as required. In Fig. 85 note the different angles of bevel to obtain the correct shape.

6. This step requires the use of the carving arbor and large and small separating discs. First redraw any important lines erased by the grinding. Now outline the detail by cutting along all the important lines with a separating disc as shown in Fig. 86. Use small, well worn discs for areas that require sharp turns. Cut through the center of the lips and above and below the eyebrows.

7. The tools used for this part of the work include small grinding wheels up to 1 inch in diameter, an 8-inch

grinding wheel, and various sizes of separating discs. Leave as is, for now, the hairline at the forehead, eyebrows, and the end of the nose. Grind between the eyebrows and the hairline, below the end of the nose, and all the area below the jaw and chin.

Use the 8-inch grinder where conditions permit and return to its use whenever possible as work progresses. Use the small grinding wheels only when necessary. At this stage of the carving, shown in Fig. 87, facial features are not clearly established. In fact, they're muddled at times. But don't despair. As material is ground away, keep the important lines visible by recutting with separating discs.

At this point it is well to compare the measurements of the original picture

Fig. 87. The carving must look worse now before it can look better. The familiar features and lines must be ground away until the correct form of the face is achieved. After this, the details of facial expression can again be carved in.

with the carving. Example: the distance between the outside of the eyes, length of nose, length of mouth, etc. Take exact measurements and correct any variance.

Facial expression is easily altered by failing to reproduce facial lines or the lip line in exactly the same curvature or form. Quite often these lines are deceiving in their appearance; a line that looks straight may have a slight curve. It's a good policy to lay a straightedge beside the line as a way of checking its curvature.

8. Additional tools used to complete the carving include a few mounted grinding stones of various shapes and dental burrs or small diamond charged tools. The hard steel dental burrs will do some very fine detail work in the eyes and ears. They wear out quickly so use them only when no other available tool will do the job.

Study carefully each small detail and continue to develop each one. The tolerance between a likeness and no likeness is extremely thin, so the subject must be repeatedly studied in every small area of detail. The shaping must proceed slowly and the results frequently studied. A final likeness, shown in Fig. 88, is dependent on the assembly of each characteristic detail.

Sand and polish the carving to a soft natural finish. Polishing is determined somewhat by the material used but, in general, a face will not accept a high polish without creating a harsh, unnatural appearance. Experiment with the clothing and the hair to obtain the most suitable finish.

Fig. 88. The finished portrait. A final likeness is dependent upon the reproduction and assembly of each characteristic detail.

Comments in General

You may reach stages in a difficult carving when you are stuck. This is most likely to occur when most of the markings have been destroyed by grinding and still no definite form has appeared. The thing to do is to study the rough stone and redraw as much as possible. This act alone helps you to revisualize the image more clearly. Continue grinding until the correct form begins to appear.

This brings us to another situation sometimes experienced. If you are at a difficult stage of a carving, if at all possible, continue working until you feel you have it mastered and have found a logical stopping place. Your time away from the work will be more relaxed and you'll start again with greater confidence.

Chapter 10

Some Notes About Display

When a few carvings have been completed and placed on a corner what-not shelf with other keepsakes, some serious thought should be given to their proper display. This planning should include the possibility of later showing them outside the home, such as county or state fairs, rock shows, or museums.

Each finished item will have required careful planning and work. In arranging its exhibit, give it the same consideration so that it can be viewed on its own merit, regardless of surrounding objects or colors. The most interesting carving can become uninteresting if simply set on a shelf with no thought given to a suitable display. And, conversely, the simplest of carvings can attain prominence if displayed properly.

Display Area

The display area or case should be well lighted and finished in a light colored non-reflective material. It should be out of reach or glass-protected from small children. Try to arrange a nook or corner for this purpose alone, so your carvings need not compete with artificial flowers, ceramics, and various novelties.

Crowding

Overcrowding is a common fault. Watch it closely. Keep it easy to look at

and displayed so that all the carvings can be clearly observed. In arranging your carvings, attempt to have each one stand out as an individual piece of work. There are many ways in which this can be done.

Display Fixtures

A simple rack or holder can be formed with small diameter wire to hold flat work in an upright position. A carefully selected small branch from a fruit tree may be used to good advantage for flowers, leaves, butterflies, or birds. Flat work also will gain prominence when displayed on a plaque or in a shadow box frame. See Fig. 89. Related subjects may also be framed and grouped into a panel for an elegant display. A background of a suitable color should be selected for each carving.

Natural, polished wood, as a base or pedestal, can be used successfully for the display of stone carvings. Driftwood, too, is especially useful because of its many shapes and textures. Always keep a proper balance between the size of the carving and the base or background used.

To prevent a cluttered appearance, small items may be grouped together to form a unit of display rather than to be scattered among larger carvings. Some design or fixture should be used to tie them together. A slightly elevated area large enough for the group works very well. Small related carvings placed on each side of a small cord or similar item can be arranged in a long or curved design that holds the viewer's interest as a unit of display.

Figures 90, 91, and 92 show an excellent way to display leaves or flower arrangements. The trees were first formed by twisting multiple strands of copper

Fig. 89. Various small jade carvings displayed as a unit on a plaque.

Fig. 90. The 168 leaves of this tree are carved from many shades of Bruneau jasper. The 18-inch tree is mounted on driftwood.

Fig. 91. Mottled green jade was selected for the leaves of this 16-inch tree. Gold plated wire, forming the branches, provides a fine setting for the leaves.

wire to form the trunk and branches. Each tree was then gold plated as a unit. A small curl at the end of each strand of wire provides a suitable mounting for cementing the leaves. A wooden base of polished walnut and a suitable piece of driftwood complete the arrangement.

If the few suggestions here help you to give thought and study to your own display our objective has been accomplished. It is an important part of the craft.

Fig. 92. An arrangement made up of gold plated wire, jade leaves, and calcite grapes.

MANUFACTURERS

The following manufacturers are included in this book as providing gemstone carving tools and equipment:

CONTEMPO LAPIDARY EQUIPMENT MFG. CO.
12273 FOOTHILL BLVD.
SYLMAR, CA 91324

COVINGTON ENGINEERING CORP.
P.O. BOX 35
REDLANDS, CA 92373

DIAMOND PACIFIC TOOL CO.
25647 W. MAIN ST.
BARSTOW, CA 92311

FOREDOM ELECTRIC CO.
ROUTE 6, 16 STONY HILL ROAD
BETHEL, CONNECTICUT 06801

WILLIAM R. HALL COMPANY
901 GIBBSBORO RD.
LINDENWOLD, NJ 08021